The Science of Self Control for Kids

Fun and Entertaining Activities for Kids to Overcome Stress and Learn Self Control Skills at Home

By

E. Kennedy

SJ Publishers

Table of Contents

Introduction

By exercising self-control, we can avoid eating the entire bag of chips or maxing out our credit cards. According to recent research, self-control is something we acquire in **preschool** and may be the difference between earning a decent career and spending time in jail.

In a recent study, Hofmann and colleagues (2013) found a connection between life happiness and self-control. Although self-control may not provide immediate fulfilment, it may instead lead to long-term enjoyment or contentment. Achievement of objectives and deferring demands are indicators of success and contentment, both likely to make us happy.

So what does a lack of self-control look like in children?

- A four-year-old frequently interrupts conversations between adults because he cannot wait for his chance to speak.

- Unable to tolerate boredom while attempting to go to sleep, a 6-year-old frequently climbs out of bed.

- When an 8-year-old's parents are not looking at her, she sneaks junk food into her room.

- A 10-year-old student plays with his pencils during free periods at school rather than completing his assignment.

- Although a 12-year-old boy claims that he wants to learn how to play the violin, he never practices.

- A friend challenges an 11-year-old to steal a candy bar from a store, and he accepts the challenge.

For years, my daughter carried about a plush orange tabby kitty. It was accidentally brought into our lives and got worn, damaged, and ragged. Many years ago, when I was a new mother, I made the rookie mistake of picking a random toy from the shop to occupy her while I looked for what we actually required — diapers and wipes. Our trip to the checkout counter proved the success of my clever plan. I had the mistaken idea that I could just put the toy away. The moment the cat escaped her grasp, sobbing started. I was forced to return it to my precious young kid when she threw a wicked tantrum (my second rookie error of the day), pay for "kitty," and escape afterwards.

This story is by no means exceptional. Even though this is my interpretation of the narrative, practically any parent and child may probably relate to the characters and minor aspects. Every parent, whether experienced or not, has experienced this kind of circumstance with their child at some point. It is a perfect example of inadequate self-regulation. Although this kind of conduct is almost expected in toddlers, self-control becomes more crucial as your child leaves home and sets out into the world.

Self-control is an essential life skill. The ability to control one's emotions is crucial for young children to learn how to control their anger or frustration. These abilities enable children to control their emotions and their actions, ideally with little help from you. Your little one can effectively cope with challenges and adapt to new circumstances if they have a strong sense of self-control.

Children who have self-regulation are better able to handle new social and intellectual demands. Self-regulation is essential in situations when children must wait their time, learn to read and interact with other kids. Your youngster would not be able to sit still, pay attention, and learn in a school without it. A student's academic performance might be impacted by inadequate self-regulation abilities.

In fact, several studies have demonstrated that kids with well-developed self-regulation abilities outperform their peers in the classroom. As they get older, these kids also tend to have higher self-esteem, higher salaries, and better physical health.

Furthermore, self-regulation enables youngsters to act in a socially acceptable manner and establish friends by helping them to control their impulses and understand the value of giving, taking turns, and correctly expressing their emotions. Self-regulation abilities can affect how effectively your kid recovers and continues to flourish in the face of hardship as they develop and age.

This book is focused on practical ways to nurture self-control in kids. It includes fun and interactive activities, strategies and worksheets to foster this life-crucial skill.

The first section of the book explains the concept and importance of self-control with stories, while the second part is full of activities to deal with thoughts, emotions and behavior. I have ensured that these activities are not boring and dull so your child can enjoy the process and use this book in his free time.

Okay, this book is great. You get it. But why would you believe what I say?

I am a child psychologist with six years of professional experience. I work with children every day to figure out and manage their psychological issues and direct them towards a healthier and happier lifestyle. One of my top priorities while dealing with these issues is teaching kids mental skills. I believe self-control cannot be skipped when teaching your children essential mental assets.

Moreover, I am a mother of three children. Trust me. I know how hard it is to teach children self-control and self-regulation skills. I understand your struggles as a mother and can help you professionally with the right tricks and resources.

So let's begin!

Chapter 1: Be COOL with Self-Control

I recall, as a small girl sitting at my grandmother's feet. She used to share tales with me about her early years as a girl. Her parents were agricultural workers. They had an extremely difficult life, yet despite their poverty, they were content.

Everybody was the same. They all worked diligently in the fields and lived solely on fish and rice. If someone managed to catch a bird, that day was filled with happiness and celebration. They would ask another family to join them for lunch. When they came upon snakes, they also ate them.

Grandmother only had a few toys. Her father fashioned a little wooden bed for a rag doll that her mother had crocheted for her. Any other toys were just broken crockery, kitchen tools, or containers that needed to be returned so they could be used to make the fish and rice.

A friend of Grandma lived nearby. She went by Lin. The two girls made up tales of adventures they had while riding their ponies. They would mount their imaginary horses with pieces of rope and gallop off to distant lands in hopes of discovering precious diamonds in caverns that they might bring back to their parents to make them wealthy. They believed that if they were wealthy, they would be able to eat food that was definitely not fish and rice but rather those eaten by kings and princes.

Snow fell one winter and lasted for a very long period. Everyone stored their rice supplies in bags and out of the reach of rodents and mice. Their salted, dried fish was strung up high, almost to the ceiling. My Grandma's mother was concerned that there would not be enough food to get through the winter. The fish was almost gone, but the rice was still holding up nicely. Soon, rice was the majority of meals. Eventually, they ran out of fish too. Grandma started to realize how much she genuinely enjoyed eating fish. Without it, the rice was so bland. She brooded about it with her mother. She said she hated eating rice without fish.

Her mother sat with her.

"Rice is really healthy for us. It sustains our life. We should be appreciative that we can eat rice. Some folks eat absolutely no rice or seafood. How do you believe they are feeling? They must be starving. Because we are not hungry, we must be happy.

"But I am sick of rice," Grandma said.

"You need to get control over yourself and stop complaining about things you cannot change. You will only feel miserable."

I questioned my grandmother if she had found how to be happy about white rice. She nodded.

"The family of my friend Lin did not have any rice or fish. Till the end of winter, they came and shared our rice. I was overjoyed to be able to feed them rice so they would not go hungry. I stopped grumbling after that. I was quite fortunate to have enough to eat, and I was happy to give some to others."

Discuss this story with your child and relate it to the concept of self-control I am about to explain.

1.1 Self-Control is a Super Power

We would be on vacation in Bermuda right about now if we got a nickel for each time we told our kids to stop bickering. Why does it feel that our kids are always grasping, nagging, punching, shouting, whining, or putting things off? Even though they make wonderful children, they occasionally lack self-control.

"Keep your hands to yourself."

Wait for your turn.

"Complete your task before playing."

"Before you act, think."

"Ask with your words rather than grabbing."

Our instructions to our children frequently focus on self-control. In order to accomplish more significant objectives, such as studying or being nice, self-control implies being able to withstand immediate temptations and refrain from acting on impulse.

Self-control is one of a set of abilities that help both children and adults regulate their ideas, behaviors, and emotions so they can accomplish their goals. This set of abilities is referred to as executive function. Children who exercise more self-control do better in school and interact with others more amicably.

We all exercise self-control in seemingly straightforward situations like waiting in line, taking turns, and sitting motionless. But self-control is a sophisticated ability that grows with practice. Self-control is something that children begin to cultivate at an early age and continue to do so into their twenties.

Children gain self-control in three areas as they get older:

- Movement regulation to prevent children from moving in unsuitable ways all the time (called hyperactivity)

- Impulse regulation helps children apply "mental brakes" and pause before acting or speaking.

- Emotional regulation so children may remain positive even when distressing or unexpected situations occur.

Self-control benefits children in all facets of life. However, it is crucial when it comes to interacting with others. Kids are more likely to fit in and make friends if they feel in control of their behaviors and emotions. Self-control does not always need exerting forceful, grit-your-teeth resolve. In actuality, self-control like that is hard to maintain over time — even for grownups. What is more beneficial is assisting children in learning and applying powerful techniques for enhancing self-control.

Self-control is a skill that we develop as we age and is not something we are born with. There are techniques to help children behave appropriately in their early years, even if they often struggle with control and delayed gratification.

The marshmallow experiment is definitely something you have heard about. When several hundred 4-year-old children were brought into the lab by researcher Walter Mischel in the 1960s, he placed them in front of a table with a marshmallow (or another reward) on it and told them, "I can give you this now, or if you wait, I will go out and do something. If you have not finished this one when I get back, I will give you another one. You can have two if you can wait. You will only receive one if you don't wait for me.

What would a 4-year-old you know do? Eat the marshmallow, or wait?

How would you respond?

In the marshmallow experiment, the researcher discovered that self-control predicted, the performance of those students in their education and careers. According to another study, self-control is a predictor of success, physical health, family stability, and even happiness. Lack of self-control is linked to drinking and using illegal drugs, being unemployed and even criminal activities.

How much restraint does your kid show? Which of the following claims about your child do you agree with?

- My youngster is persistent in her activities.

- My kid anticipates things.

- My kid is focused and pays attention.

- My youngster considers before saying or behaving.

- My kid reacts to logic.

If you agree to any of the above statements, your kid probably already has high self-control.

- What do you think about these claims?

- My kid is stubborn.

- My kid cannot wait to get something.

- My kid breaks down under minor strength.

- Little inconveniences cause my youngster to overreact.

- The unexpected nature of the surroundings makes my youngster uneasy.

Your youngster is probably less capable of exercising self-control if you indicated "yes" to any of these questions.

Here's the good news: We now understand that self-control is flexible as a result of decades of research. Some people develop strong self-control as early as possible. Some people develop greater self-control as they become older. Most significantly, regardless of their starting point of restraint, most people can learn to practice more restraint.

First, let me give you a detailed insight into why you should teach your children self-control.

1.2 Fly with Your Red Cape

Self-regulatory behavior is essential for success in all aspects of our lives, from controlling impulsive behavior to mastering the art of delaying gratification and managing emotions when encountered with conflict and discomfort. Since kids with bad self-control frequently display more behavioral issues than their self-disciplined friends, teaching kids self-control is more crucial than parents may realize.

Let's go deeper into the advantages of self-control.

- **Improved Emotional Intelligence**

  Emotional navigation is a challenging process that frequently influences one's decisions and behavior. Children are prone to be persuaded to create new viewpoints and adopt new actions as they investigate the world around them.

  According to recent studies, having strong emotional intelligence might help one work creatively even when they have a creative block. By participating in activities that use imagination, a youngster can dramatically improve their problem-solving abilities.

  Additionally, a vivid imagination helps foster a more upbeat mindset. A person with numerous ideas would consider other perspectives rather than just one, opening up possibilities and various paths to accomplishment. Positive children tend to have better attitudes, resulting in improved conduct in the present and future.

  Self-confidence may be increased by having emotional intelligence. Self-confidence can help people succeed in various contexts, according to a study published in The National Academies Press. Competent leaders frequently exhibit self-assurance because they are aware of their own development and sensitive to the demands and goals of their team.

  Your child may establish lasting relationships and forge deep connections with others around them when they possess emotional intelligence. Children are more likely to gain the trust and respect of their peers if they are empathic toward them. A University of Wolverhampton study found that youngsters with high emotional quotients also have an easier time making and maintaining new connections and have more positive interactions with others who are different from them.

- **Improved Stress Management**

  According to studies, kids and teenagers today are more anxious than ever. Young people now experience significantly higher levels of anxiety and stress as a consequence of the pressures of education, important examinations, social life, sports, or other hobbies, as well as spending a lot of time in front of screens.

  For our kids, we cannot entirely get rid of stress. Additionally, protecting your youngster from life's challenges won't be in their best interests. Raising a resilient child who can overcome difficulties and obstacles is far more effective.

  Greater self-control may enable a person to control their anxious thoughts better, reducing their intrusion and overwhelming nature. Additionally, those who have high self-control are more adept at placing themselves in circumstances that advance their objectives and emotional well-being. Therefore, those with high self-control avoid potentially stressful situations more effectively than those with poor self-control.

Although it might seem obvious, there have not been many researches that have looked at the relationship between self-control and stress, and the majority of those studies have only looked at American college students. Therefore, we studied over 4,000 people from various socioeconomic backgrounds in Poland, Germany, the United States and Sweden in order to ascertain the association between self-control and stress.

As was to be predicted, those with better self-control reported much lower levels of stress than those with less self-control. Additionally, each of the four nations experienced this.

- **Boosted Academic Performance**

Successful people must be lifelong learners who can properly evaluate their learning and who are metacognitive about the continually changing environment. Kids who lack the capacity to retain tenacity and focus their attention will continually be pushed right and left by their initial inclinations inside the educational system. Additionally, kids who do not understand self-evaluation techniques would not be able to focus their attention on the areas that really need it. Self-control enables learners to manage these settings by finding solutions that work, even if some students may view tough books, complex lessons, or bad study surroundings as insurmountable challenges.

- **Improved Ability to Make Decisions**

  Making decisions is made simpler because of self-control, which is one of its advantages. For instance, a person who loves chocolate may need to show restraint and avoid chocolate bars, pastries, and sweets due to high blood sugar levels.

- **Reduced Temptations**

  Being able to resist temptation is one of the advantages of having self-control. We can easily be persuaded to do actions that will distract us from our objectives and lower our quality of life.

  For instance, if we do not exercise frequently, we may feel pains, exhaustion, and other health issues on a regular basis, in addition to problems in later years of life.

- **Improved Relationships**

  Not only are persons with self-control in control of their activities, but they are also in control of their emotions. They are able to regulate negative emotions like envy and hate as well as their rage. Compared to those with less self-control, they are better able to handle interpersonal connections because of this.

- **Increased Likelihood of Success**

  Self-control makes it harder for someone to get easily sidetracked. They can better manage their time and resources as a result. They frequently work diligently and consistently to achieve their objectives, which increases the likelihood of success.

- **Better Performance**

  Self-control also aids pupils in performing better on tests and maintaining mental acuity. Compared to their counterparts, they are more committed to accomplishing their objectives. Similar to this, those with strong self-control may focus their time and effort on being successful at work by being productive there.

Do you not think these benefits are worth it for your child? So let me help you.

Chapter 2: Change Your Thoughts, Change Your World

A disciple and his master were once strolling through a forest together. The fact that the disciple was restless always concerned him a lot.

"Why are most people's minds restless, and only a few have a tranquil mind?" he questioned his teacher, "What steps can I take to calm their mind?"

"I will tell you a story," the instructor added, smiling at the student.

"On a lovely day, an elephant was munching on a tree's leaves as it provided shade. A little fly buzzed in and quickly perched on the elephant's ear. The elephant ignored the fly and carried on eating calmly.

The fly buzzed loudly as it flew around the elephant's ear, but the elephant appeared unaffected. The fly was perplexed and said, "Are you deaf?"

The elephant said, "No!

"Why do you not care about my buzz?" The fly asked.

"Why are you making such a racket? Why can you not remain still for a bit?" asked the elephant, chewing leaves peacefully.

"Everything I see, hear, and feel impacts my behavior," the fly responded.

"What's your little secret? How do you manage to maintain such composure and stillness when I buzz in your ear?" asked the fly.

"My five senses do not disrupt my peace, so I can continue eating happily."

"How is it possible?" inquired the fly, puzzled and surprised.

"I do not allow them to control my attention. That is why." The elephant replied.

"Since my thoughts and my mind are within my control, I can focus them where I choose and block out any distractions, even your buzz," the elephant added, "I am totally absorbed in the act of eating, savoring my meal, and happily digesting it."

The disciple's eyes widened and a smile spread across his face as soon as he heard these remarks. "I have finally understood," he remarked, turning to face his teacher. If my five senses and everything that occurs in the world around me have influence over my mind, then my mind would constantly be in a state of continual turmoil. On the other side, my mind will become quiet if I have control over my five senses, can ignore sense inputs, and can manage my thoughts. I will be able to ignore its restlessness and experience calmness.

The teacher said, "Yes, that's correct. The mind is restless and wanders wherever the focus goes. You can master your thoughts if you master your attention."

Discuss this story with your child and share examples of thoughts with each other.

Try to picture a life without a thought if you can. It would not be much of existence for a person. Every waking minute is filled with thoughts, whether they are insightful, uninteresting, humorous, or odd. It is also undeniable that thinking is something that we do instinctively. We might say that thought is to humans what flying and swimming are to birds like eagles and dolphins.

But thinking is one thing, and understanding the nature of cognition is quite another. The majority of us do not fully comprehend the nature of thought, just as eagles fly without understanding aerodynamics and dolphins swim without understanding fluid mechanics. Thoughts concerning cognition itself are much less prevalent than the act of thinking itself.

Our ideas, views, and beliefs about who we are and the world around us are known as mental cognitions or thoughts. They consist of the viewpoints we bring to any scenario or encounter that skew our perception (for better, worse, or neutral).

An attitude is an example of persistent thinking. Attitudes arise as a result of repeated and reinforced thoughts.

Thoughts are typically controlled by conscious awareness, despite being molded by life events, heredity, and education. In other words, you have the option to manage or mound your ideas and attitudes if you are conscious of them.

2.1 My Strategy Toolkit

Humans have 12,000 to 70,000 thoughts in a day. Some of them are beneficial, some are enjoyable, some are unimportant, and some might linger in our brains and interfere with our activities.

Children express their views in various unusual ways. Kids have described ideas as an "annoying voice" in their heads or as "like there's a goodie and a badie," and it can be difficult to decide which to listen to. This is especially true with persistent and unhelpful thoughts. It can be challenging to assist children in first recognizing and then comprehending how ideas might have an effect on them when they are still learning about metacognition or thinking about thinking.

How we feel, and act might be influenced by our thoughts. The tone of our internal dialogue can influence whether we react to a situation with serenity, anxiety, or anger. Think about your 10-year-old receiving an invitation to a friend's party. Since the birthday girl enjoys dancing, one of the listed activities on the invitation implies that a dance lesson will be held that day. The invitation causes your 10-year-old to think,

"Yay, a birthday party!" and, "Oh, I'm not good at dancing," "I can't dance at the party," "Everyone will be better than me," "Everyone will laugh at me," "It's not fair," and "Why does it have to be a dance party." Your 10-year-old transitioned from being thrilled to feeling uneasy to furious. And then avoidance behaviors may come next, such as claiming she doesn't want to attend the party or is unwell that day. If your 10-year-old verbalizes her ideas, you have the chance to comprehend her internal monologue and assist her in problem-solving. However, kids aren't always able to verbally express their thoughts to others.

Negative ideas that frequently cross our kids' minds are called nagging thoughts. Additionally, they may not be advantageous to their mental condition. In the previous example, it is possible that your 10-year-old keeps thinking, "Everyone will laugh at me." It is set off during swimming lessons, show and tell, and physical education classes. And when it does, it has the potential to override her internal monologue and have an effect on her emotions, self-assurance, and behavior. It is a persistent, useless notion that could require assistance to disappear.

The best techniques to deal with persistent thoughts vary according to who is thinking about them. Some people think it is preferable to call attention to them, while others try to ignore them, while still others choose to ignore, challenge, or let them pass. As a child psychologist, I've discovered that there isn't a one-size-fits-all approach to helping kids deal with persistent negative beliefs. Some children truly enjoy acting as "thought detectives" and delving into their beliefs to gather proof that will ultimately question and alter their viewpoints (a cognitive-behavioral therapy approach). Others, on the other hand, would rather act as objective spectators and perceive their ideas as passing objects in a type of visual imaging (e.g., floating on leaves down the lake, an acceptance-based approach). And many people choose to use a variety of tactics according to the circumstance.

So, even though there are many strategies to deal with nagging ideas, I have discovered that helping youngsters learn to let go of their thoughts may be quite beneficial. Let's see some strategies.

Strategy: Help Recognize the Difference between Positive and Negative Thinking

It can be difficult for children to distinguish between negative and correct ideas.

Using stuffed animals to symbolize each school of thought is a quick and easy technique to assist young children in making the distinction. The happy bear and the irritable puppy may be considering the same event—not going to the park because of rain—but have completely different perspectives on it.

If your youngster is older, make a line down the center of a sheet of paper. Write "Negative Thoughts" or "Meany Brain Thoughts" on one side. Write "My Good Thoughts" or "Smart Thoughts" on the opposite side.

Strategy: Help Put Distance between Oneself and Negative Thoughts

Helping your youngster get "some distance and perspective" on a situation is also crucial. Avoid implying that they are being negative in your response. Blame the "negative brain" instead. As a result, you become a supporter in your efforts to protect your child from this "troublesome third party of thoughts — the true bad guy destroying her day."

This renaming "begins to demote the legitimacy of negative thinking, urging the kid to not believe it as the "truth," but as the obtrusive, distressing, overprotective, or just generally uninformed voice that it is."

Ask your kid to choose a name for their critical mind. Here are a few instances: Mean Mouse, Mr. Sad, and Fun Blocker. Ask them to illustrate the character and give it a voice. Additionally, they can come up with creative responses to that pessimistic mind: I'm not listening to you; you make me feel lousy, and you need new spectacles. "You're not in charge of me."

I have an idea of how to start the conversation with your kid about developing the bad-brain character. You may respond, "Remember when you called me dumb because I accidentally sketched on the table? Right now, you don't feel that way. What, though, would you call the voice in your brain that initially gave you that impression?

The objective is generally not to suppress, resist, or stop unpleasant ideas. We must alter how we interact with them: Even if the negative brain is wired to focus on the drawbacks, shortcomings, and disappointments, we may still get up and see things from a different perspective. The concept is only one possible interpretation of a tale; by choosing to think about just one or two of the possibilities, you can escape the moment in which you feel stuck.

Strategy: Help Kids Acquire a Positive Outlook

In order to combat negative thinking, it is essential to instill optimism in children. Imagine that two little children are enjoying rocky road ice cream when the cone for it slides off. It was not placed correctly, so it dropped and someone yelled, "I want another one!" "Why does this constantly happen to me?" says the other youngster, "I hate this shop. Everything is ruined. This is the worst day of my whole life."

In the first instance, the upbeat youngster presents the information and sees a way to resolve the issue. The pessimistic youngster inserts superfluous material from outside the script, giving intention, permanency, and a global quality to something that was a tiny accident, pure and simple.

The "Unfortunately, Fortunately" game can be played by parents and their children. Create "five sticky situations" with your youngster, which you then write out on cards and place in a hat. Each individual then takes a card from their deck and reads the tragic circumstance. Sadly, the movie I wanted to watch was sold out, for instance. The other person replies, "But happily, I went to watch another movie," or anything of that effect. Then you switch off, stating both unfavorable and advantageous factors.

The next time your kid faces a challenging circumstance, you may say, "There are many 'unfortunatelys' building up. Can you look for any 'fortunatelys' in this scenario?

I hope these strategies will help your child be in more control of their thoughts. Let's move on to some worksheets.

2.2 My Worksheet Treasure

Kids might develop negative thinking habits too. These could happen more frequently during stressful moments, and it is simple to be judgmental of oneself and concentrate on the negative ideas. Sometimes we may catastrophize an event, making it appear worse than it actually is, or we may take responsibility for situations outside of our control.

The resources listed below could be helpful for kids.

Help John

Hi kids! Let's have our first worksheet. It is John's first day at a new school. He is having negative thoughts that are making him feel anxious. Can you help him change his negative thoughts into positive ones?

Negative Thoughts

I don't have any friends here. No one is going to like me!

My friends at my old school are having fun without me.

I'm so nervous! The kids will probably think that I'm weird.

This school is SO big. I know for sure that I'm going to get lost!

When I am an Angry Bird...

This worksheet will assist you in figuring out your thoughts and behavior when you are mad. Here we go.

WHEN I FEEL ANGRY

I THINK....(What are some thoughts that go through your head whenever you feel angry?)

I SAY....(What are some things you say to others whenever you feel angry?)

I DO....(What are some behaviors you display whenever you feel angry?)

_____   _____

_____   _____

_____   _____

What are some things you can think, say or do instead?

Worry Balloons

This worksheet will help you understand what you are worried about as we all know, worry and stress make you lose control of your thoughts. Then you can let go of the balloon of worry and watch them fly off.

What am I worried about?

You Belief-o-Meter

Just having a thought does not mean it is true or that we have to believe it. Write some of your thoughts in the bubbles, then use the dial to rate how much you believe each thought.

Put Your Thoughts on Trial

In this exercise, you will put an idea on trial by playing the roles of prosecutor, defense attorney, and judge to determine the thought's accuracy.

Prosecutors and Defendants: Collect evidence for and against the notion you had. Evidence may only be utilized if it can be verified. There will be no interpretations, speculations, or views!

Judge: Make a decision on your thought. Is the idea correct or fair? Is there anything else that could explain the facts?

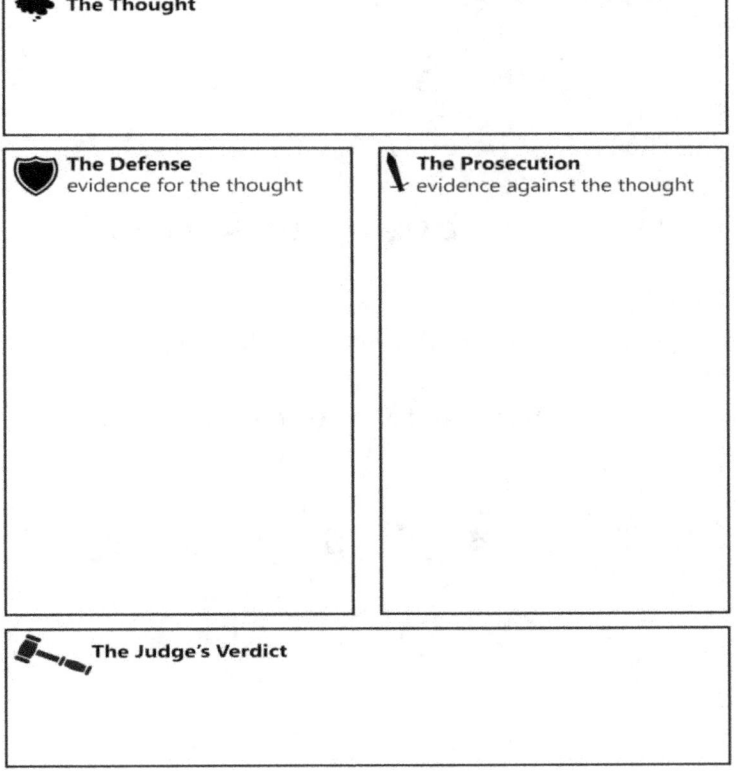

What are ANTs?

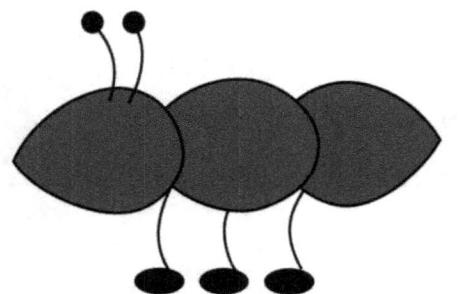

Automatic

Negative

Thought

How hard does your ANT bite?

How much does this ANT impact your feeling or behavior?

How hard is it to cope with this ANT?

1__2__3__4__5__6__7__8__9__10

ANTs are negative and random. Sometimes they pop into our minds out of nowhere.

Here are some examples of ANTs:

- **All or Nothing:** Thinking something is ALL good or ALL bad.

- **Always/Never:** Thinking something ALWAYS or NEVER happens without considering the times it does not.

- **Feeling Thinking:** Thinking that it must be true because you feel a certain way.

- **Disaster:** Thinking everything is the end of the world or the worst thing ever.

- **Telling the Future:** Assuming the worst will happen without all the facts.

- **Labelling:** Thinking of yourself or someone in negative terms.

- **Mind Reading:** Assuming you know what someone else is thinking or feeling.

Your Self-Esteem Badge

Write your name in the circle. Then write 6 positive self-talk statements or positive traits that you have. Look at this badge when you are feeling down to remind yourself how special you are and stop negative thinking.

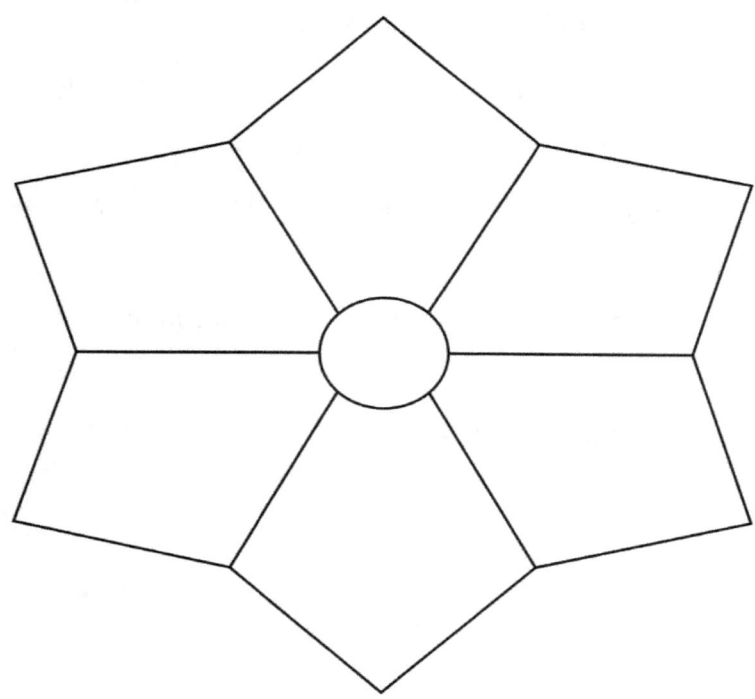

Switch Yourself OFF

This exercise will help you point out your negative thought and stop it in your tracks before it does any more harm. Write your observations in the free space under point 3 and the things you are grateful for under point 4.

My Off Button

1. Notice your negative thought

"I CAN'T DO IT"   "IT'S ALL MY FAULT"   "I'M NOT WORTH IT"   "I'M NOT ENOUGH"

"NO ONE LIKES ME"   "I'M NO GOOD"   "IT'S TOO HARD"

2. Take five full breaths

- Place your right hand index finger at the base of your left hand thumb.
- As you breathe in and out through your nose move your right hand index finger up and down your left hand thumb and fingers in five full breaths.

Finger Breathe

3. Let go of your negative thought by noticing three items around you

- What is the item called?
- What colour is it?
- Where is it in relation to you?

4. Smile to yourself in a moment of gratitude

"I take care of myself"

"Nice one"

"I notice my thoughts"

"I did it"   "I am kind to myself"

INNER CHILD YOGA

2.3 My Activity Box

Remember, minds get good at what they do. Your brain develops negative thinking "channels" if you keep thinking negatively. You risk making this style of thinking your default. Your brain is hardwired to produce negative ideas if you think a lot negatively. Your mind only sees the negative in everything.

According to King's College London research, persistently thinking in a negative way affects your brain's capacity for thought, reasoning, and memory formation. It essentially depletes the resources of your brain.

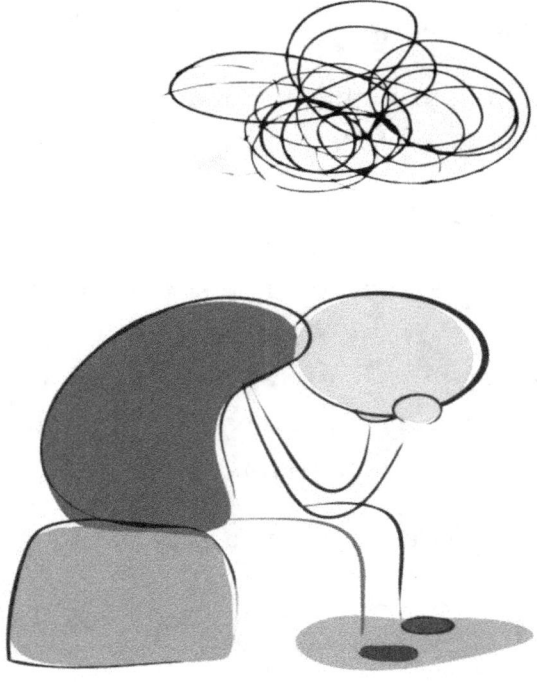

Here are some activities for your kids.

Shoot Thoughts through a Basketball Hoop

Children may put their ideas through a basketball hoop by taping them to a ball or writing them on paper. It could take place on the basketball court outside or inside as a set-up. Kids will love releasing the ball as they try to shoot the hoops.

Feed Thoughts to an Anxiety Eater

Younger kids might want to feed their anxious ideas to worry eaters. Making a worry eater out of a tissue box and other craft materials is the first step in this project. Kids can feed the worry eater images of their fears or text that their parents have written.

Use a Container or Cup to Crush Thoughts

Children who are older might want to crush milk bottles and soda cans in the recycling to let go of negative thoughts.

Fly the Thought Balloons Away

Ask your youngster to reflect on a persistent thought that has been bothering them. Create some of your own examples to assist in illustrating. A typical worry-inducing thought can begin, "What if...?" (For instance, what if I forget the words to my speech, what if I am late for school, etc.)

Then, inflate a balloon as big as you can or have your child inflate a balloon for you.

Ask your youngster to write their views on the balloon using a permanent pen. They can draw a picture, or you can aid them if they don't want to write or are too young to write.

Then release the balloon.

It will thrill your youngster to see it soar around the room.

Then, when they go to take it up, the printed message on the balloon becomes smaller.

It is a terrific idea to talk with your child afterwards about how they felt after letting go of the concept. How did it feel to see it fly off and become small as it moved far away? Maybe they have shrunk in their head as well? Discuss which of the alternative ideas your child comes up with regarding the situation—for example, "I can only try my best" or "maybe it won't be so bad"—might be the most useful idea to pay attention to.

Flush the Thoughts Away

Ask your youngster to jot down a notion on a piece of toilet paper, similar to the prior suggestion. Ask your child to write a word, an idea, or an image of anything they'd like to "let go" of with a pencil and then have them watch it get flushed down the toilet.

Some kids like to scream their words into the toilet bowl, flush them away, and then repeat them. Children who need to let out some of their energy or stress from their thoughts (such as "it's not fair") may find this useful.

Children will find it entertaining to see their thoughts vanish.

In the next chapter, we will talk about emotions and how thoughts affect them, leading to bad behavior.

Chapter 3: Surf Your Emotions like Waves

Once there was a child with a very bad temper. His father trying to help him, handed him a bundle of nails and instructed him to pound a nail on the fence whenever he was angry.

Because the child was always upset, he found himself pounding tens of nails every day. But as time went on, he hammered less and less. He thought it was simpler for the child to let his anger go than to pound nails all day.

When he had used up all the nails, he went to his father and said, "Father, I'm out of nails." But I don't believe I need them right now. I'm much better at controlling my anger than I used to be."

"That's good," his father responded. "However, I want you to remove every nail you pounded." Please inform me when you are finished."

So his son began pulling out the nails he had pounded during the previous weeks and then called his father. "Tell me what you see, son," his father asked as he approached the fence.

"It's the fence." It no longer appears as good as it previously did. There are now far too many holes."

"You're correct, son. We might be able to fix it if you only hammered one nail. But you've pounded far too many. You've been enraged with your mother, your friend, and everyone else around you. You uttered things that upset them. As a result, you began to lose the people who cared the most about you."

His father went on.

"If you keep hammering nails into the fence, it will be beyond repair." Even now that you can manage your fury, you won't be able to restore the fence to its former glory. The holes will always be there and are not easily repaired."

His son grasped the message. He did not want to live a life where he lost the individuals he cared about the most. And, while he could not do much about the fence then, he could start taking care of what was left so that he did not damage it any further.

The Moral of the Story

Your outbursts of rage may last only a few seconds. However, the consequences of your actions might endure a lifetime, especially for people who are always around you. Consider the impact of your actions on them.

The same goes for every other emotion.

You need to manage your emotions so you can get the most out of life, avoid stress and keep healthy relationships.

So let's get some strategies on the subject.

3.1 My Strategy Toolkit

At first, look, managing our own emotions appears to be a simple task, but it is actually rather difficult, especially for developing children and teens. It entails recognizing your feelings, managing stress, employing appropriate coping skills, problem-solving through dealing with problems, and knowing when to seek assistance. This might be a lot for developing kids and teenagers. They do not always know how to handle their emotions, which is why adults must give guidance along the way. So here are a few strategies for your child to practice.

Strategy: Remind Yourself that Hurting Others is Never Acceptable

Establishing clear rules for what is and is not acceptable is critical. We are not permitted to harm others or damage someone's property in our home. This involves inflicting harm on others through our words.

Strategy: Use Your Words to Express How You Feel and What You Want to Happen

Recognizing significant sentiments acknowledges that these feelings are valid and essential, and expressing what they want to happen helps to initiate a problem-solving discussion. Of course, what they want will not always be an acceptable solution for all parties, and this can be a difficult lesson for children to learn (and virtually impossible for very young children to learn), and they will often require assistance to work out a more peaceful solution, especially if they are used to striking out when they feel strong emotions.

Strategy: Take Three Deep Breaths or Count to Ten Slowly

Helping youngsters realize that these strong emotions are totally normal but that their reactions and actions as a result of those emotions might harm others (and, ultimately, themselves) is a vital element of the cool-down strategy. Taking some deep breaths or counting to ten slowly allows the youngster to recognize their body's warning indicators, such as tense muscles, clenched teeth, or a racing heart. Talk to your kid about how their body feels when they are upset or agitated, and then present the notion of taking a few breaths to collect themselves and establish a better course of action than lashing out at another person while forming a plan.

Strategy: Ask for Input Help in Resolving the Problem

As an adult, I frequently find that talking through an issue helps me process it, and children will also want assistance as they learn to problem-solve and discover answers in social circumstances. Allow your child to ask for help when they don't feel they can solve the problem on their own, and keep these important lines of communication open so that one day when they are dealing with much bigger issues than a squabble with a sibling or frustration with a friend, they know they can always come to you for assistance.

Strategy: Take a Break

Tell your kid that sometimes the offered solution is insufficient, that they may still feel angry or sad after going through all of the above steps, and that in these cases, it is sometimes preferable to move away or find another safe approach to defuse those feelings.

Moreover, if you suspect your kid is about to engage in potentially explosive behavior, letting him or her take a little break from whatever is distressing them might help the child calm down and behave appropriately. It also provides a secure space for the youngster to breathe and possibly speak with a parent about the experience.

Below are a few tips for parents to help kids regulate their emotions:

Strategy: Calm Down

Have you ever heard the expression "Put on your own oxygen mask first"? This also pertains to remaining calm. If you can learn to calm yourself down when your child is upset and model an acceptable reaction, they will learn to cope. You can be a sounding board, but if you become too upset yourself, you are not assisting them in learning to calm down. Always take a pause before responding. Be matter-of-fact and businesslike, allowing your child to work through his emotions before directing him to what he has to accomplish. Listen to him, but do not prolong the problem by giving in to him.

Strategy: Your Reaction Matters a Lot

Do not downplay or make your youngster feel as though his feelings are "wrong." Some parents struggle with their child's emotions on the opposite end of the scale. In reaction, they may try to convince their child that their emotions are incorrect, asking things such as, "Why are you sobbing over this? That's ridiculous!" or "Are you upset about that?" Allow them the room and respect to coping with their feelings on their own, even if it appears ridiculous or as if they are overreacting. (This does not give them license to misbehave or treat the rest of the family poorly.) It simply implies that kids should be allowed to process their feelings on their own in their room, for example.)

Strategy: Figure out the Triggers

Consider the following questions:

What are the most common situations for your child that set him off? What irritates you?

What are his or her triggers? What are they? (Are they the same thing?)

Which categories would you place the majority of your buttons in? What about your kids?

Here are a few examples:

- Approval

- Pride

- Injustice

- Autonomy

- Respect

- Envy

- Shame

Once you have identified your child's triggers, inform him of what you've discovered. Then you might ask him, "How can you behave differently the next time?" How can you respond responsibly the next time you think something isn't fair, rather than striking the wall, shouting and swearing, or smashing things?" Make your youngster come up with some responses. Consider asking him to make a list of things he can do the next time he is triggered.

Strategy: Reflect on their Feelings

Listening and reflecting back to the kid is part of providing a caring and welcoming atmosphere for youngsters to communicate their feelings. Instead of telling a youngster, they should not feel a certain way, it is best to mirror the emotion using terminology to communicate the experience appropriately. Instead of saying, "Don't say you don't like your sister!" a parent can say, "It seems like you're upset with your sister right now." "Could you tell me how you're feeling?" This method helps the youngster to talk about his or her feelings and consider good ways to deal with them.

Strategy: Lead by Example

Setting a good example is maybe the essential thing a parent can do to assist their child in regulating their emotions.

Because children frequently imitate their parents' conduct, it is critical to demonstrate adequate emotional control. We educate our children to do the same by effectively managing our emotions.

In addition to the strategies mentioned above, there are several practical things parents can do to assist their children in dealing with emotions, particularly challenging emotions like anger or fear. These allow a youngster to express their displeasure without endangering themselves or others.

Let's discuss the practical section of the chapter.

3.2 My Worksheet Treasure

The intensity of strong emotions can be overpowering. They might be terrifying or cause behavioral and relational problems. The contrary can be tough as well; many people learn to suppress their emotions or are unaware that they are experiencing them. This can lead to troubles in the future.

Emotion worksheets are a tool that you may use with your children to help them understand and manage their emotions.

I Spy

This worksheet will help you understand and label emotions. There are five different emotion faces in the worksheet. Fill all faces of one category with a color of your choice.

Emotion I Spy!

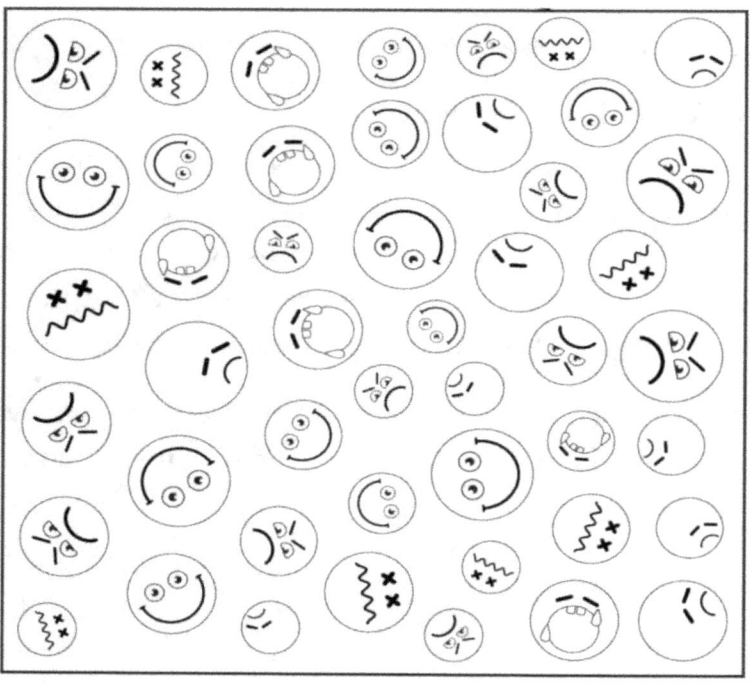

What is Your Feeling Forecast?

This worksheet will help you get in touch with your inner self. You are asked to mark the rainbow with the intensity of your feelings. The higher you put your mark, the more intense your feelings will mean. Fill up the boxes in the end with effective coping mechanisms.

FEELING FORECAST:

When we are calm and ready to learn
we are like a rainbow

When we want to storm off, we are like a snowstorm

When we feel like we need to scream
then we are like a thunderstorm

Color the rainbow below and
put an x where your feelings are now

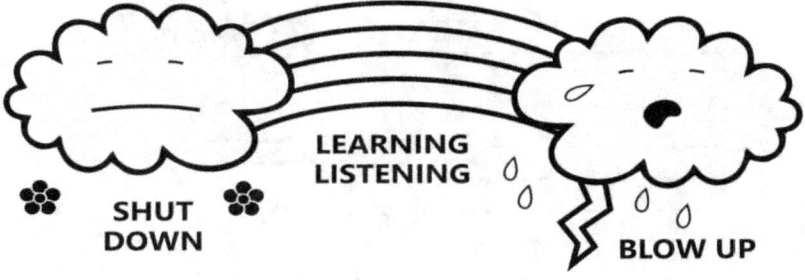

LEARNING
LISTENING

SHUT
DOWN

BLOW UP

When my feelings are snowing or raining
these things help me get back to the rainbow

When You Are Red

This worksheet will help you determine your anger triggers and understand your thoughts, feelings and behavior with consequences. In the end, you will find a breathing exercise.

Things that make me angry

What makes me angry:

_____

_____

_____

_____

My thoughts:

_____

_____

_____

_____

My feeling:

_____

_____

_____

My behavior:

_____

_____

_____

Consequences:

_____

_____

_____

_____

STOP

Breathe

Hold: 4 seconds

Breathe: 4 seconds

Breathe: 4 seconds

Hold: 4 seconds

Worksheet: My Coping Sheet

This worksheet will help you find a solution for feeling a certain way. Let's go through it step by step.

HOW TO WORK THROUGH YOUR EMOTIONS?

Name The Emotion

• I felt like _____
  (describe in a few words)

Identify The Cause

• I was _____(where)

• I remember noticing

  _____

Challenge The Emotion

• Was my _____ (feeling) appropriate to the situation?

• Is this situation a distress that I can control?

• If it is out of my control, is this a distress I have to accept and tolerate

Identify The Behavior

• When I felt _____.

  I_____(behavior, action)

• What I wish I had done

  was_____.

I am Anxious

This worksheet is best used when you are feeling anxious and worried. It will take you through the process of exploring the causes and signs of anxiety and then some coping skills.

I Can Cope! with feeling ANXIOUS

Some things that make me feel anxious are......

1. _____

2. _____

3. _____

These changes happen when I feel anxious:

Changes in my body...	Thoughts I have...	Things I do...

When I feel anxious, I can cope by:

Check all of the coping skills that might be helpful! Use the blank spaces to write in your own

☐ Deep breathing   ☐ Going to walk   _____

☐ Using positive self-talk   ☐ Writing in my journal   _____

☐ Meditating or relaxing   ☐ Practicing mindfulness   _____

☐ Talking to a friend   ☐ Thinking happy thoughts   _____

☐ Talking to an adult   ☐ Keeping myself busy   _____

☐ Playing a game   ☐ Exercising   _____

I can Express My Feelings

This worksheet will help you share your feeling with others and includes prompts to do so.

Feelings Expression Prompt

Use this worksheet to help you express your feelings to someone!

_____ (their name).

I am feeling _____ . (Are there any other feelings that you are experiencing. Use

the Feelings Bank to help you identify more feelings _____ _____)

I feel this way because (What did they do that made you feel this way)

_____

_____

_____

I have been feeling this way since _____
(How long have you been feeling this way)

I wanted to let you know how I feel because (why did you want to share your feelings with them)

_____

_____

I'm hoping that (What do you want to happen after they hear your feelings) _____

_____

_____

Thank you for listening to me!

FEELINGS BANK

Unhappy	Shocked	Frustrated	Disgusted	Scared	Misunderstood
Angry	Hurt	Embarrassed	Unsafe	Sad	Insulted
Disrespected	Disappointed	Annoyed	Ashamed	Betrayed	Excluded
Offended	Upset			Annoyed	Anxious

Shoo Shoo Stress

This activity needs you to fill in the boxes and realize what is causing you stress so you can avoid it and just focus on what lies in your domain.

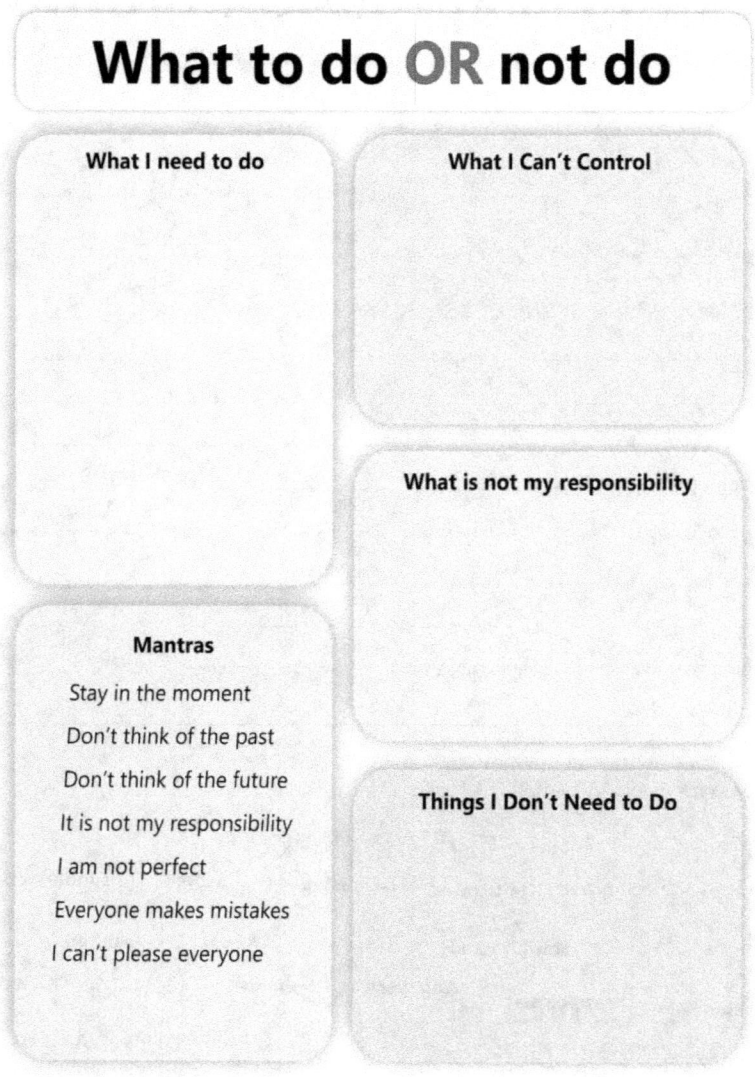

What to do OR not do

What I need to do

What I Can't Control

What is not my responsibility

Mantras

Stay in the moment

Don't think of the past

Don't think of the future

It is not my responsibility

I am not perfect

Everyone makes mistakes

I can't please everyone

Things I Don't Need to Do

Check in with Yourself

This exercise helps you understand what you are feeling and get in touch with yourself.

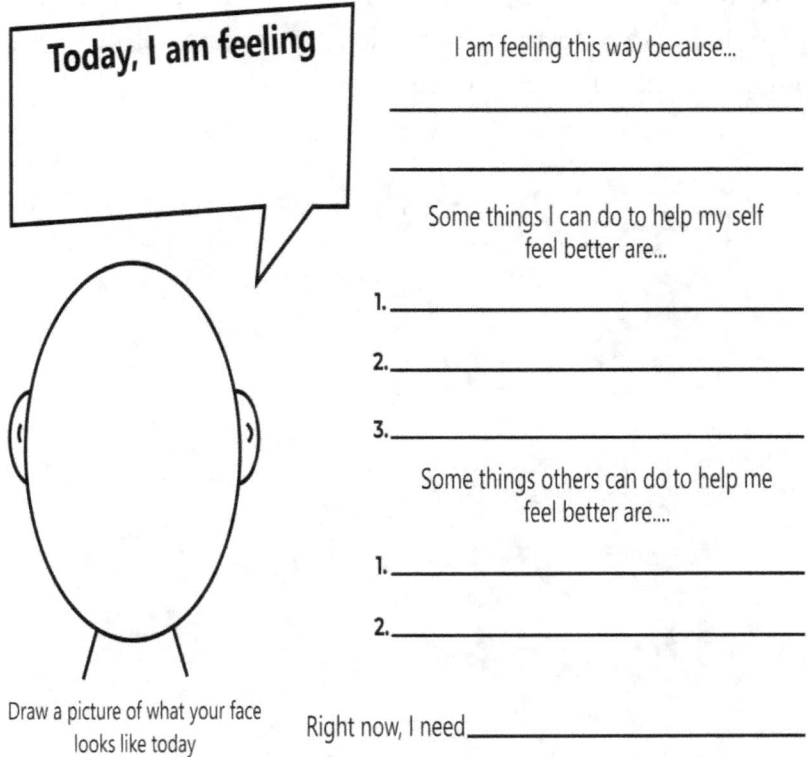

How are you feeling today?

Today, I am feeling

I am feeling this way because...

_____

_____

Some things I can do to help my self feel better are...

1._____

2._____

3._____

Some things others can do to help me feel better are....

1._____

2._____

Draw a picture of what your face looks like today

Right now, I need_____

I hope you enjoyed it! Now let's move on to activities.

3.3 My Activity Box

Today, too much is going on in the world. We may all benefit from additional support and coping skills. There are various reasons why children may have powerful and hard sentiments, whether it is a frightening current occurrence in our world or an issue in their own personal life. While adults require help in dealing with their emotions, children and teenagers require it much more.

It is crucial to remember that children's minds are still developing. According to science, the brains of children and adolescents are evolving. Their "thinking brain," or prefrontal cortex, falls behind their limbic system, or "emotional brain." They can't always reason their way out of unpleasant situations on their own. This indicates that children will require additional assistance, guidance, and experience handling difficult emotions when they arise.

Feelings ID

This project is an excellent place to start when educating young children about emotions. Here's what you should do:

- Make a list of your emotions. Begin with a fundamental emotion, such as happiness or sadness, and explain that it is a feeling. Give a second example using a more complicated emotion, such as excitement or surprise. Ask students to produce more sensations, add them to the list, and show the list on chart paper or with a projector for students to see.

- Determine if your feelings are positive or bad. Return to the beginning of your feelings list and ask the kids to give you thumbs up for feelings that make them feel good on the inside and thumbs down for feelings that make them feel bad on the inside.

- Engage in a follow-up conversation. Ask kids whether they have ever had sensations when they couldn't decide whether they felt nice or bad on the inside. Please provide an example.

Perform a Full-Body Scan

This exercise requires your youngster to sit or stand motionless and close their eyes. Then, beginning at the top of their heads, ask them to pay attention to any feelings they are having. If their head feels normal, have them continue to focus on their face, shoulders, chest, arms, hands, and so on, all the way down to their toes.

If kids reach a point where they recognize a distinct sensation, such as a quickly pounding heart or feet that sense the desire to tap or bounce, that's fantastic! Your kid may then link those experiences with the work they accomplished in their emotions bank to correctly label the emotion. According to research, even brief periods of this type of meditation can help children become more resilient and capable of coping with powerful sensations when they emerge.

Dice Game

Using translucent acrylic picture cubes, make "feeling dice" — slide drawings of faces displaying distinct emotions on each side. (Instead of sketches, you may use images or magazine cutouts.) Allow each youngster to roll the dice in a small group. When the dice lands on a sensation, ask the youngster to name it and explain a moment when they felt that way.

Act it Out

If your child is naturally theatrical, they may benefit from acting out various emotions, similar to a game of charades. Allow them to choose the name of emotion from a hat or basket, and then see if you can predict the feeling they're acting out.

What Would You Think If...

Consider some frequent events that may generate various emotions. Here are a few examples:

"Your grandmother picked you up after school and drove you to the ice cream shop."

"A classmate splattered paint over your artwork."

"Your mother screamed at you."

"Your brother wouldn't let you use the swings."

Put different situations in a hat and pass it around the circle or small group while music is played. When the music stops, the youngsters holding the hat should choose a scenario (you may assist the child read it if they can't yet). Then, ask the youngster to express how he or she would feel if the situation occurred to them.

Now was it not that fun? Let's move on to the next chapter.

Chapter 4: Your Behavior Empowers You

Have you ever questioned why you keep repeating a particular action or why you feel the way you do? If so, allow me to throw some light on the subject by describing the connection between ideas, feelings, and behaviors.

Our ideas produce feelings, and our feelings influence our conduct. Let us look at a basic example. If I prefer being outside near water and swimming, the prospect of going to a pool makes me joyful. These thoughts and sentiments will motivate me to organize swimming-related activities. On the other hand, my companion will avoid swimming if the notion of being near water frightens her. The identical experience (swimming) seen differently by each of us (thoughts) results in distinct emotions (joy or fear), which leads to diverse behaviors (going to the pool or not). Neither of us is correct or incorrect. We simply have different opinions about what is (or is not) entertaining!

Take some time to ask yourself what you feel if you make the same decision over and over. Determine the feeling. Slow down and pay attention to what you are saying to yourself if you are furious. How do you talk to yourself? What are your thoughts on the folks involved? What are your convictions? What are your core beliefs? Once you recognize your thoughts, you can assess whether or not they are realistic. Perhaps your perception is exaggerated or obscured by previous encounters. Change your thinking to be more objective and evidence-based. Chances are, even minor changes in your thinking will have an effect on your emotions. That effect might just be a reduction in the strength of the feeling. This may be enough of a difference for some people to influence their decisions.

Below is an example of how your thoughts, emotions and behavior interlink.

Situation: A kid says something mean to you at school.

One possible thought

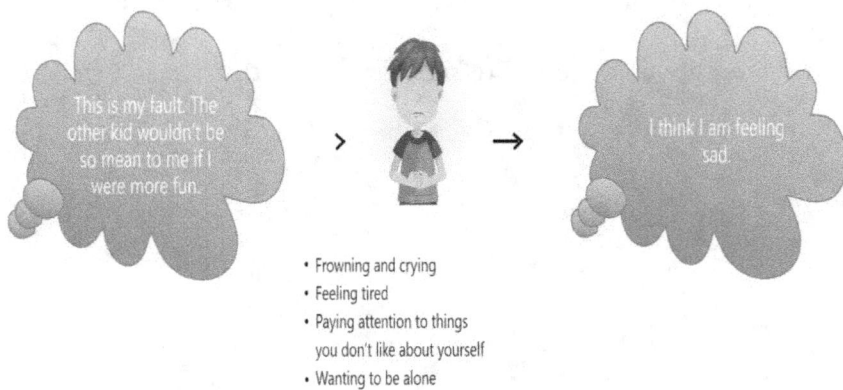

This is my fault. The other kid wouldn't be so mean to me if I were more fun.

I think I am feeling sad.

- Frowning and crying
- Feeling tired
- Paying attention to things you don't like about yourself
- Wanting to be alone

Another possible thought

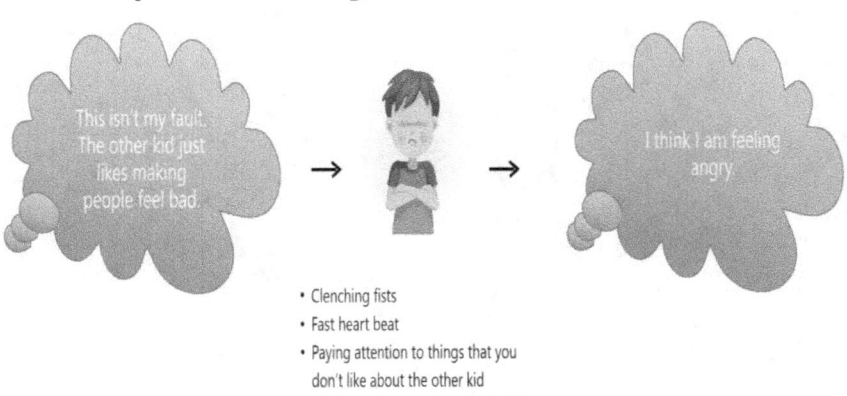

This isn't my fault. The other kid just likes making people feel bad.

I think I am feeling angry.

- Clenching fists
- Fast heart beat
- Paying attention to things that you don't like about the other kid
- Wanting to be mean to the other kid

Insanity is defined as doing the same thing over and over again and expecting a different outcome. Although the term "insanity" may not be the ideal option, it does convey the message that continuing certain behavior while expecting a different consequence would undoubtedly result in irritation and misery! Make an effort to become more conscious of what you are telling yourself. You may discover that you have the ability to modify behavior merely by changing your thoughts. Give it a go!

To conclude, if you follow the strategies in the last two chapters, half of your work is already done on self-control.

Now let's have some strategies for behavior management.

4.1 My Strategy Toolkit

Being a parent is important in helping shape your children's behavior. It may be both tough and rewarding. While it might be difficult at times, a few essential ideas can help.

Strategy: Establish Clear Behavior Expectations (Specific, Observable, Measurable)

When children understand what good conduct entails, it is much easier for them to adhere to the rules. Uncertain expectations can lead to doubt and worry; after all, youngsters will understandably believe it is unjust to be reprimanded for failing to obey an unclear norm.

Remember that children are still learning what good conduct entails, so they require a lot of specifics: "Be kind to others," may be too abstract for toddlers, while "let everyone take turns," refers to an actual action they can perform that you can objectively assess.

At the same time, you do not want to overwhelm them with so many rules that they can't remember them all. Find an age-appropriate mix between specificity and generality, and assist children by providing concrete examples and visual aids.

Strategy: Solve Issues with Your Child

On days when your child struggles to manage their behavior, talk to them about how they can do better the following day. For example, ask your child what occurred and express your desire to assist them in doing better in the future.

Strategy: Maintain Your Cool

Talk calmly with your youngster and get their feedback on what might be beneficial. Using a problem-solving approach might make kids more eager to express their feelings.

Strategy: Inquire about What they are Working On

Occasionally, children can plainly explain the rationale for their conduct. For example, your child may disturb their school class because they are bored. The option might be to urge your child's teacher to give them more difficult homework.

Strategy: Check to See If They Require More Assistance

Misbehavior might also result from a lack of knowledge about how to accomplish the job. Kids will occasionally choose to seem "bad" rather than "dumb." To avoid being mocked by peers, they may choose to act out rather than ask for assistance.

Strategy: Display Your Emotions to Your Youngster

Telling your child how their behavior affects you honestly allows them to recognize their own feelings in yours. And starting sentences with 'I' allows your youngster to see things from your point of view. 'I'm unhappy because there's so much noise and I cannot talk on the phone,' for example.

Strategy: Get down to Your Child's Level

When you grow close to your child, you might pick up on their emotions and thoughts. Being near to your child also helps them focus on what you're saying regarding their behavior. You don't need to make your youngster look at you if you're near to them and have their attention.

Strategy: Choose Your Fights Carefully

Before you become involved in whatever your child is doing, especially to say 'no' or 'stop,' consider whether it is truly important. You generate less potential for conflict and ill sentiments by reducing instructions, demands, and negative criticism to a minimum. You may use family rules to communicate to everyone what is most essential in your family.

Strategy: Give Kids Responsibilities - And Consequences

As your child grows older, you may offer them greater responsibility for their own actions. You may also allow your youngster to face the natural repercussions of his or her behavior. For example, if your child is responsible for packing for a sleepover and forgets their favorite pillow, the logical result is that your child will have to sleep without the pillow for the night.

Other times, you may be required to impose repercussions for incorrect or undesirable behavior. Make sure you've communicated the penalties and that your youngster has consented to them ahead of time.

Strategy: Be Adamant about Not Whining

When you give in to your child's whining about something, you may unintentionally train your youngster to complain even more. 'No' means 'no,' not maybe,' so say it only when you mean it.

Strategy: Keep a Sense of Humor

It is frequently beneficial to make daily living with youngsters light. This may be accomplished through the use of music, comedy, and fun. You could, for example, play the threatening tickle monster who demands the toys cleaned up off the floor. Humor that makes you both laugh is fine, but humor at the cost of your child will not help. Young children are vulnerable to parental' teasing.'

Strategy: Prepare for Difficult Situations

Meeting your child's needs and accomplishing the things you need to do might be difficult at times, such as while you're out shopping, in the vehicle, or at an appointment. You can arrange around your child's demands if you think about these difficult circumstances ahead of time. Give your youngster a five-minute heads-up before requiring them to switch activities. Explain to your youngster why you require their participation. Then your youngster will be ready for what you anticipate.

Below are some tips for parents. This type of behavior by parents is absolutely unacceptable:

- Do not nag or bring up negative conduct too frequently. Nagging is ignored by children.

- Do not call names.

- Do not criticize your youngster.

- Do not label your child as "bad." Only the behavior is inappropriate.

- Do not spank. Spanking teaches your youngster that hitting someone to solve an issue is OK. It is ineffective, and you may endanger the youngster. When you are angry, never slap a youngster.

- Do not scold too frequently. Scolding causes anxiety in youngsters and may cause them to disregard you. It may also aggravate the behavior. Never reprimand your child while they are in time out.

- Do not yank your child's hair, grab his or her arm, or shake him or her.

I hope these strategies clear things up. Next, we have worksheets for the kids to work on.

4.2 My Worksheet Treasure

The way someone conducts themselves is referred to as their behavior. It refers to their activities, emotions, and functioning in response to daily contexts and events. Challenging behavior refers to behavior that interferes with a child's daily existence. We need to educate children to value self-control and to make sensible decisions (without being zealous about controlling everything), so they may learn to regulate their behavior, perceive challenges as opportunities, and stay healthy, happy, and wise.

It is worksheet time for the kids!

You Know What Happens When You...

This activity will help you point out the consequences of your actions so you become more self-aware and leave unhealthy behaviors behind.

Directions: Write as many consequences as you can (positive or negative) for each action.

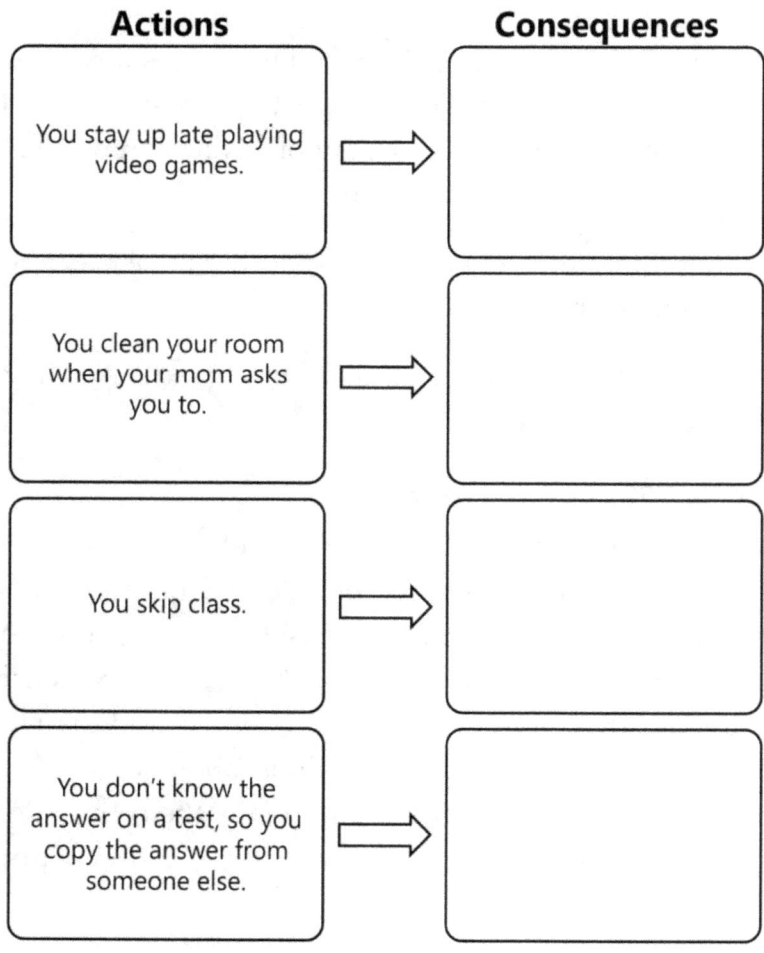

Actions

You stay up late playing video games.

You clean your room when your mom asks you to.

You skip class.

You don't know the answer on a test, so you copy the answer from someone else.

Consequences

Who is the Responder?

This worksheet will help you calm yourself down when you are feeling anxious by doing or saying the things your anxiety response friend will do or say to yourself.

The Anxiety Respond-er!

If there was a person who could respond perfectly whenever you're feeling anxious, what would they say or do to help you calm down?

What's that Behavior?

This worksheet includes categorizing your behavior into mindful or unmindful to help you better understand good behavior.

Mindful or Unmindful

Directions: Read and circle the Mindful actions

Leaving your jacket on the floor when you come in from outside.

Keeping your voice quiet when other people are reading.

Helping someone who is hurt or scared.

Crossing the street without looking

Letting someone finish talking before answering.

Practicing a new skill like sports or music until you feel your body improving.

Journal it Out

This worksheet needs you to fill out your behavior choices for the day and improvement plans for the next day. So let's go.

My Behavior Journal

Did I reach my behavior goals form yesterday?

☐ **YES** (AWESOME JOB!!)

☐ **NO** What kept me from reaching my goals?

_____

Good behavior that I displayed today:

_____

_____

Poor choices that I made today:

_____

_____

How did these choices affect myself and others?

_____

_____

My behavior goals for tomorrow:

_____

_____

What do I need to do to reach these goals?

_____

_____

What Triggers a Mess?

This exercise will help you explore the reasons you behave the way you should not so you can work on your triggers.

Soft Drink Triggers

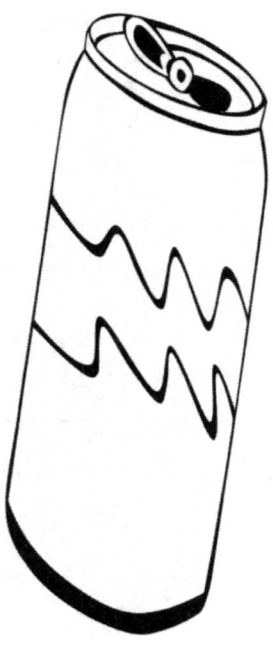

This bothers me a lot. I want to explode.

This bothers me a little bit.

This does not bother me at all

Behavior Detective

This worksheet is all about behavior understanding. Come on, grab a hat and get to work, detective!

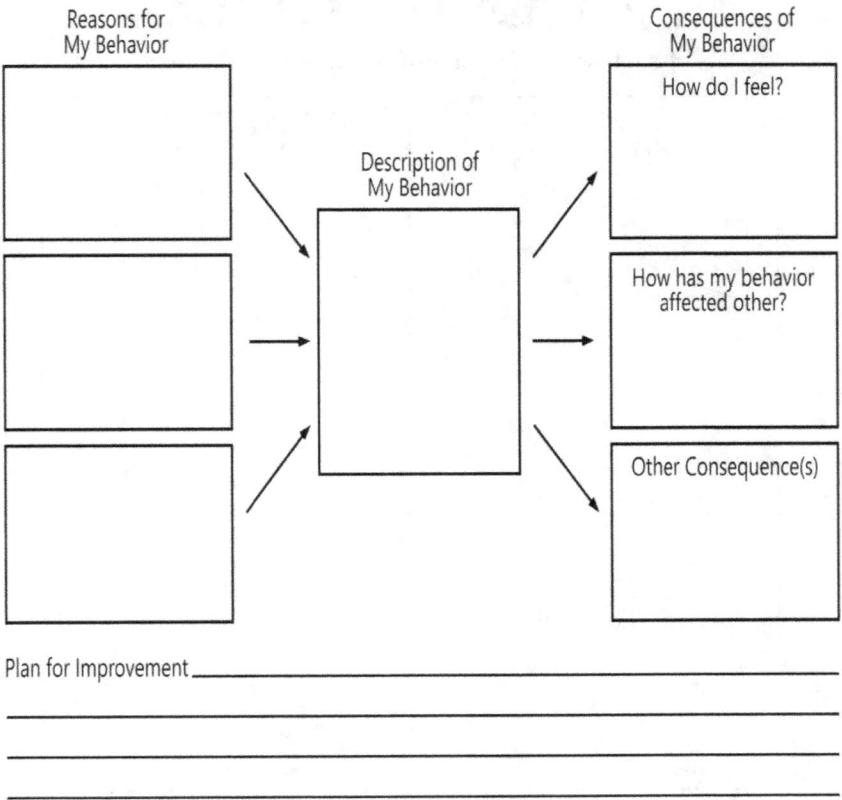

Behavior Reflections

Reasons for My Behavior

Description of My Behavior

Consequences of My Behavior

How do I feel?

How has my behavior affected other?

Other Consequence(s)

Plan for Improvement _____

_____

_____

_____

Sort it, Little One!

This exercise requires you to cut the cards below the table and then stick them up inside the table as self-control or no self-control behavior.

SELF-CONTROL SORT

Read each scenario and cut them out Then sort them

Shows Self-Control	DOESN'T Show Self-Control

You are so excited you scream loudly.	Your feelings are hurt so you write a letter.	You get angry so you throw your book against the wall.	You wait patiently to eat desert until your mom says it is okay.
You are feeling angry so you slam the door.	You yell "I need to use the bathroom" while your teacher is talking.	You are excited about something so you tell your friend about it.	You are upset so you talk back.

Beat the Monsters

This worksheet needs you to understand and then beat your worry monsters. Have fun!

That's it for the worksheets. Now I have some activities for you.

4.3 My Activity Box

Having a child that has behavioral challenges may be difficult. Parents may find themselves unprepared to deal with the difficulty of a disruptive youngster. If you have a kid with behavioral issues and are seeking strategies to regulate that behavior at home, the following suggestions may be useful. When children begin to feel out of control, these creative activities can help them feel calmer, more focused, and more empowered.

Feelings on Paper

Give your youngster a blank circle or face sketched on a sheet of paper. Then have him sketch a picture of how he feels when he is furious. Repeat the practice with emotions such as happiness, sadness, fear, frustration, jealousy, and so on. Having your kid consider and explain what feelings do to a person can help him connect with what he is truly feeling, which can help reduce outbursts that occur when he is struggling to cope with unpleasant emotions.

Tap the Balloon

This entertaining game requires only some balloons and an open area. Arrange kids in a circle and divide students to two teams alternately (one student is team 1, the next student is team 2, the next kid is team 1, and so forth). Make a circle out of balloons. "Team 1!" exclaims the captain. "Only team 1 kid should tap the balloons. Switch to Team 2; only Team 2 kids should tap the balloons. Switch on and off at 20-30 second intervals. Kids will have to pay close attention to the audio signal that indicates it is their team's turn to tap.

Want to include everyone in fun? Make use of colorful balloons. When the "off-limits color" is spoken out, no one should tap any balloons of that hue. Then change the colors! Students must listen for the aural trigger and suppress urges when the forbidden hue appears nearby.

Make a Rewards Menu

Positive reinforcement of good conduct is one of the most effective methods of encouraging children with behavioral challenges to behave appropriately. Create a "menu" of prizes from which a youngster may pick when he behaves well or completes a job without whining or becoming sidetracked. Some possible rewards include being able to pick what to eat for supper, having an extra half-hour of television time, or receiving a special snack or gift.

Breath into It

If your child has behavioral or anger concerns, a breathing exercise or guided meditation will help calm him down. When your youngster is having a tantrum or is having difficulty focusing on a task, have him sit on a yoga mat on the ground or in a chair and close his eyes. Then, take him through a guided meditation to help him refocus and breathe. Ask him to picture his favorite spots on the planet, such as a summer camp or a beach. Then, request that he imagines what he feels, sees, smells and hears. A meditation session can take five to thirty minutes and help angry children feel more cheerful and calmer.

Activity: The Obstacle Course

This is an excellent method for practicing impulse control, balance, response time, and self-regulation. When you say "green light!" "the children begin to move through the hurdles. Call out "yellow light" to emphasize that the youngsters should go slowly through the obstacles. "Red light!" exclaims someone and that's their cue to freeze - even if they're perched on the edge of a cliff!"

Clap Pattern

This is a simple and enjoyable group game that requires no props. Your youngster must mimic your clapping beat, and each child adds to the clap pattern. This game requires a minimum of three players.

The first player begins by clapping.

The second player follows the first player's clap. Then he adds his own pattern.

The third player should begin with the first person's clap, then the second person's clap, and then add his own pattern. This will continue until one of the players breaks the pattern.

I wish you all the best of luck in being your best version and acquiring effective self-control skills!

Conclusion

The need for self-control might sometimes feel like a ruse, which is unfortunate, but its effect is enormous. Significant research done over three decades has discovered that children's self-control as five-year-olds is one of the best predictors of their future health, wealth, and success. Knowing how to teach children self-control can lead them to success.

Self-control refers to the ability to manage one's own behaviors and emotions in order to achieve a long-term objective. Delaying pleasure, managing urges, pushing through irritation, sticking with a difficulty, waiting patiently for your turn, and regulating emotional outbursts are all examples of self-control. By the age of 10, most youngsters appear to have mastered self-control.

Children who lack self-control are not stupid. Impulsive and risk-taking individuals have tremendous strengths. They are frequently our discoverers, adventurers, entrepreneurs, or innovators. They can cause a lot of problems too.

Self-control is intimately related to decision-making. A lack of self-control as a youngster may result in a little too much fun food at the party, spending more time gaming than doing homework, or throwing a few tantrums. In the near term, these actions' consequences may appear minor. Nobody's world has ever come crashing down because they ate too much cake on a Sunday afternoon. However, the repercussions of poor judgments and a lack of self-control throughout adolescence may be severe in the short and long term.

When our children reach adolescence, we will have little control over their experiences. This is where kids learn about themselves and their place in the world. At this point, their self-control is important. Adolescents who lack self-control are more prone to make judgments that limit their chances and lead them to a more dangerous lifestyle. These include health decisions (drinking, smoking, food, sleep), financial decisions (gambling, reckless spending, choosing play over work), and behavior (relationships, study, work, addiction etc.)

Self-control will be crucial in shaping their decisions, experiences, and the way their brain develops as they grow into adults. Childhood self-control builds self-control in adolescence, which prepares the brain for complicated life challenges.

I hope this book has helped your child gain self-control and take part in more positive behavior.

www.ingramcontent.com/pod-product-compliance
Lightning Source LLC
Chambersburg PA
CBHW071115120626
46546CB00003B/1349